MAR 1 5 2016

W9-CLY-468

JOURNEY TO THE CROSS

by Shane Cloonan

ISBN: 978-1-5136-0350-6

DEDICATION

This book, my first book, is dedicated to the memory of my grandmother, Maureen Cloonan, who touched the heart of everyone who knew her, but none more than me. And while she never saw the completion of this book, her spirit and unconditional love helped me write every page. I remember how excited she was when reading the first draft—so excited that she sent a copy of it to her native Ireland.

Much love always . . .

ACKNOWLEDGMENTS

This book would not have been possible without the help and unconditional support of my parents, who saw its potential before I did. I can never thank them enough for their love and guidance, not only with this book, but in everything I do. Also, for keeping me mostly on schedule, and for the balance they taught me to have in my personal life. They both have sacrificed a lot in their lives so I wouldn't have to sacrifice anything in mine.

I'm forever blessed.

I also want to thank Mr. James Blake of St. Anne Parish School, Barrington, for fueling the ongoing passion I have for creative writing.

I would like to thank my art teacher, Mr. Richard Browning, for his beautiful drawings. They are what made my writing come alive.

I wish to thank the following people for their contributions to this book: Deb Anderson of Anderson Graphics, who did the graphic design. Also, Linda Wolff and Sue Samuelson, who edited the narrative. And James Harvey of James Harvey Photography.

Last, but certainly not least, I would like to express my sincere gratitude to my publisher, Mr. George Rawlinson, who helped turn my dream into a reality.

PUBLISHER'S PROLOGUE

Every once in a while, just reaching out and shaking someone's hand starts a remarkable journey. It was that way with Shane Cloonan, who is about 45 years younger than I am. Those years aside, Shane is an incredible young man. And his debut book speaks volumes to the talent and tenor that define who he is.

Shane's wonderful writing turns this simple story into a richly emotional experience, especially appropriate for younger readers. He combines engaging characters with a resonant sense of Christian history. From cover to cover, his writing will wrap those younger readers in its message of commitment, service and salvation, showing them that as they grow and change, God will always be there for them.

Great art is timeless. It assumes a new relevance to each generation, connecting the past, feeding the future. I saw that frame of reference in the art of Richard Browning, an area artist and art educator who has lived in the Fox Valley for more than forty years.

I am deeply grateful for his extraordinary artistic contributions to this book. His drawings visually capture, compress and encapsulate Shane's narrative.

We hope that this book finds the audience it deserves.

PUBLISHER'S INTRODUCTION

Take your child or grandchild on a *Journey to the Cross*. It's an imaginative tale told by the Jesus donkey, an improbable fictional creation engagingly brought to life through the words of 14-year-old author Shane Cloonan.

Shane's book began years earlier, starting with his lifelong love of nature. When he was a young boy, Shane had two pet donkeys, as well as other unusual animals, including chickens, pygmy goats and a guinea pig. The donkeys were kept and cared for in a barn adjacent to his family home. Shane noticed that these two donkeys, named Burt and Biscuit, had crosses on their backs. Each cross had a dorsal stripe of darker hair down the length of the back, then crossed by a stripe across the top of the body at their shoulders. Shane wondered why? Why a cross? Well, he did a little research online, learning there's a Christian allegory about the cross on a donkey's back—that it's said to be the inherited shadow of the cross as a donkey stood at the crucifixion when Jesus died, a reminder that one of the world's humblest creatures carried Jesus at various times throughout his life, from Bethlehem to Calvary, so to speak.

In reward for the loyal and unassuming love of the donkey, God ordained the shadow of the cross to fall across its back and the donkey has carried the cross ever since as a sign that the love of Jesus carries a reward for everyone to see.

According to a Christian website, most, if not all, donkeys have the narrow strip of hair that makes the shape of a cross. Some, however, are more visible than others.

Shane used this simple visual as the basis for a compelling journey—a *Journey to the Cross*.

ike all great stories, mine will be remembered forever. Let me start by telling you that I'm a donkey. I'm also going to tell you about the most important event in my life . . . the most important event in history.

One morning I was inside the barn, eating an ordinary breakfast in my ordinary stall.

But there was something about this morning that made it seem very fateful, although I knew that whatever was coming was nothing to be afraid of.

At the time, I did not know what was coming, or where it was coming from. But I could sense the presence of something much more powerful, and a lot bigger than you or me.

But I just kept my focus on the hay that the barn keeper fed me each and every morning.

I was still eating my breakfast when I heard a small sound outside—a sound that crept closer and closer to me. I then heard the clank of the sliding bolt unlock, and my stable door swung open, slowly and quietly. I looked up and saw Joseph, who looked anxious, maybe even a little nervous. It was a look I had never seen from him before.

He stepped closer, then whispered in my ear, "We must go," he said, quickly handfeeding me the last of my breakfast.

About a million different thoughts ran through my head.

Go?

Go where?

Joseph slipped on my halter, carefully attached the lead and walked me out into the cool, crisp air and the sounds of an awakening world.

The next thing I knew, Mary placed a beautiful blanket across my back. The blanket had a cross stitched on it. As Mary turned toward Joseph, I could feel a warm glow across my back, as if something inside of me was starting to change.

Did the cross that was stitched on this blanket symbolize something? Once we were ready, Joseph helped Mary climb up on my back. Then he gently pulled me toward the bright morning sun, which, over the next few hours, would rest like a gentle palm on the back of my neck.

heard Mary say to Joseph, "It's a long way to Bethlehem." I had a strange feeling, almost overwhelming, that this would begin a lifelong journey for me—a journey that meant more than just travelling from one place to another.

Halfway through our journey to Bethlehem, my hooves had become sore and my legs were shaking, but I knew I had to keep going. I had to keep going for Joseph, but I had to keep going for Mary most of all. She was a fine young woman, pure of heart and always faithful to God.

Tired or not, we would make it to Bethlehem.

It was just before arriving in Bethlehem that I heard Mary say to Joseph, "I can feel the baby coming!" Joseph started going from inn to inn, knocking on every door, hoping to find a place to stay. But time after time he heard the same thing, "I'm very sorry, there just isn't any room for you today."

Mary pleaded, but no one would take them in. She knew her child would be very special because of the angel who had come to her earlier in a dream. He had said, "The child who will be born to you is the Son of God. You shall call him Jesus."

I didn't know that I was carrying the unborn Son of God, of course. But I did feel something special. So I kept the faith and trudged along the rough terrain as quickly as I could. I knew it would soon be getting dark and, with the baby coming, Mary needed a suitable place to stay.

We finally arrived at a stable that looked very much like my home. I wondered why Mary and Joseph would stay in such a place, which was fine for me, but not comfortable for them.

That night, Mary gave birth to her son. Joseph lit a lantern and made a bed for them in the manger, gathering up clean hay put there for the animals. Mary wrapped Jesus in the wide strips of cloth she had brought from home.

From the very first time I saw Mary's baby, I knew this was truly an extraordinary moment. He was the most beautiful baby I had ever seen. His face was sweet and serene, but strong, too. Then, suddenly, it came to me. This was the Son of God. Our Savior had indeed been born.

A dove was cooing, and all the other animals in the stable stared with a sense of wonder. The evening sky opened up, and a heavenly light poured down upon the stable. The light came from a very special star.

ary stared silently at her baby son, who was wiggling and blinking his eyes in the lantern light, just like babies do. She was filled with awe.

Other people noticed things, too. Three kings from the east had seen that special star in the night sky. They were very powerful people, yet they would immediately travel to honor the baby Jesus, their Lord, our Lord.

"Where is the child who was born last night?" they asked after arriving at the stable. "We saw the star announcing his birth. Now we have come with gifts to worship him."

They brought gold, frankincense and myrrh.

All I could feel was pride, but the humble kind of pride you feel when you're grateful for something, like a prayer that has been answered. I did wonder, though, if people knew how "important" I had been in the birth of the world's new king, the King of Kings. I stopped myself right then and there. My importance did not matter. It did not matter at all. Our Savior had been born. And that's what mattered most. That's what mattered more than anything and everything.

Visitors who had come to offer prayers dropped to their knees and bowed in the dusty stable for the Christ child. I was reminded of the significance of what had just taken place.

I may have been only a little donkey, but inside I felt bigger than the biggest camel. I had helped carry the Christ child.

But I didn't have time to think about all that had happened. Or to wonder if any of this would have happened without me.

Visitors sat and stayed for hours, eventually leaving long enough to let Joseph get some rest. After he fell asleep, an angel appeared to him in a dream.

"You must get up," the angel said. "You must take the Christ child and his mother to Egypt where they will be safe."

Evil King Herod had heard of Jesus' birth. He said that there would be no other king to worship while he was still alive.

Joseph helped Mary climb atop my back. She held the little baby Jesus closely in her arms. I would carry them to safety, following every step of Joseph's lead.

Even though we were in a new land, I returned to my normal boring life, doing the little chores I was accustomed to, like carrying things here and there for Joseph, all the while feeling blessed to be part of something so special.

Then, some years later, King Herod died. Another angel appeared to Joseph in another dream. "When you wake up, take the child and his mother and return to your home," the angel said.

"It is safe to go back to the land of Israel."

With Joseph again in the lead, I carried Mary and Jesus back to Israel and they made their home in Nazareth in Galilee.

Jesus grew up strong and healthy and learned the carpenter's trade from Joseph, until the time came for him to do the work that God had given him to do.

I remember the moment that Jesus left home. I understood, of course, but it still hurt not having him to myself every day.

Many years later, I awoke one morning to the sound of footsteps inside the barn. I saw a man with loving eyes and long brown hair. I realized the baby that I had once carried on my back had returned.

esus led me out into the damp field, talking to me all the way. After he fed me some apple slices as a treat, I realized my journey was not yet over. It really had just begun. I felt the same glow on my back as I had years earlier, only it was noticeably stronger. I was nervous, but I knew as long as I was with Jesus, I would be all right.

We would set off for the familiar town of Jerusalem. Having traveled the same roads before, I remembered the steep mountains that we passed. They were the same mountains people passed on their way to Bethlehem.

e stopped several times along the road, which was often just a dusty path. Even so, all types of people would gather around whenever Jesus stopped. Most people just wanted to hear what he had to say. They wanted to hear the word of God. But other people came looking for one of his miracles.

Religious leaders at every temple and the men who would be kings were afraid of Jesus. They were afraid that so many people were worshipping him. They became jealous and said Jesus was a threat to their authority.

esus knew that danger awaited him in Jerusalem, but he knew he had to go anyway.

When we entered the city, I couldn't imagine what would happen next. Things seemed okay at first. As I walked through the streets of Jerusalem, with Jesus on my back, people came and spread out their cloaks or laid leafy branches on the ground before us. Shouts of "Alleluia" echoed everywhere and rose to the heavens.

We traveled to the Temple in Jerusalem. Trouble started there. Even though I was tied to a post near the outside door, I could hear people talking inside. The Temple authorities knew that a great many people were spellbound by what Jesus said.

The authorities were determined to crucify Jesus. How could this be? What were these men doing with our King, the King of Kings?

The High Priest and other Temple officials questioned Jesus for many hours, trying to find a reason to have him crucified.

One of the officials asked, "Are you the Son of God?"

"I am," said Jesus, knowing his answer, though honest, would determine his fate.

"Crucify him," they shouted.

"Crucify him," was their final verdict.

I felt confused, as if the world was spilt in half. I had seen so many men and women worshipping Jesus, but now they taunted him. I didn't understand these people. And I didn't know what to think anymore.

A group of Roman soldiers pushed Jesus out of the Temple and beat him on the street. They put a filthy cloak on him and piled a crown of thorns on his head.

"Now the 'King of Kings' has his own crown," one of them laughed.

They placed a heavy wooden cross on Jesus' shoulders and told him to carry it up a mountain, which was so high it looked as if it could pierce the clouds.

I was able to pull my lead from the post I was tied to and free myself. But I did not run away. I followed Jesus up the mountain. Each time I tried to get close to him, the Roman soldiers pushed me away. I wanted Jesus to put the heavy cross on my back, then I would carry it for him.

ut what could I do? I knew I had to face the truth. Even though I had tried to help Jesus carry this burden, I was pushed away again and again. So I decided to just follow along as best I could.

After watching him beaten, bruised and kicked, the crowd, myself included, finally arrived at the face of a mountain overlooking Jerusalem.

Shane Cloonan is an Elgin resident and high school freshman.

This is his first book.